It's All About Me

An Interactive Guide to a Happier,
More Fulfilling and Successful Life

GERALD M REICHE

BALBOA.
PRESS
A DIVISION OF HAY HOUSE

Balboa Press books may be ordered through booksellers or by contacting:

Balboa Press
A Division of Hay House
1663 Liberty Drive
Bloomington, IN 47403
www.balboapress.com
1 (877) 407-4847

Printed in the United States of America.

ISBN: 978-1-4525-1418-5 (sc)
ISBN: 978-1-4525-1419-2 (e)

Library of Congress Control Number: 2014908203

Balboa Press rev. date: 7/24/2014

ACKNOWLEDGEMENTS

There are so many people to thank and acknowledge for this creation. Kathy, you are the love of my life. You have always supported me in any endeavor. I could not be more grateful to have you in my life. Linnaea Mallette, thank you for showing how limitless the human spirit can be. Thank you to my family for your support and your patience and the endless hours of listening. Thank you Mary Ritch for your work in making all of this presentable.

PREFACE

Congratulations! By picking up this book you have taken the first step in making a positive change in your life! Let's get started with a question.

How many times have you read a story or listened to an interview or watched a program about someone who came up with a very simple idea, or who wrote a best-selling book or sang something or performed in some way that made them rich and famous?

How often have you found yourself saying: "Man, I could do that just as well as that person, or even better if I only had the chance," only to find yourself walking away or turning the channel in frustration because the voice in the back of your head said:

"That could never happen to me."

Why do you think that is? Is it because you have less talent? Is it because you do not know the "right people?" Is it because you do not have enough time or money or knowledge or education? What is it about you that is so different that *your* dreams go unanswered while you watch *others* get everything they want and, seemingly, without effort? The answer may surprise you, but I assure you it is absolutely true. It can also be summed up in a single word:

NOTHING!

That is right, I said "nothing!"

I have probably never met you, spoken to you or even heard anyone mention your name, and yet I can tell you right here and now that you are just as smart, just as talented and just as capable of being successful as anyone!

So, what's the problem? Why aren't you as happy, successful and fulfilled as you believe you ought to be? That is what this book is all about.

There are hundreds of programs, self-help books, audio recordings and "get rich" gurus who are very eager to sell you on how to be healthy, wealthy and wise.

These programs go into great detail about how unsuccessful your attempts at improving your life have been and how their new miracle discovery is going to lead you to salvation. They compare you with others who have made it; they talk about others' journeys and how modeling yourself after those wonderfully successful people will bring you fortune and fame. Then they relate the success of all of those other people to their own story and try to convince you that their own journey to success is exactly what you can expect, if you follow the "new and improved" model that they have developed just for you! Sound familiar?

So, how many people do you know who have tried a program, or two, or three, but are still struggling, do not understand why they are still struggling, but continue to buy the books, attend the seminars and focus on the success of others? Can they explain why the last program did not work? Can they explain how the next one will?

Most successful people teach from the premise that, if it worked for them it should work for everyone else. Unfortunately, what most of these people and programs fail to consider is that this "what's good for the goose is good for the gander" mentality tends to ignore the most important element of any successful program, thus dooming it to failure. That element?

YOU!

You are a unique individual. You have your own thoughts, feelings, beliefs, hang-ups and issues. You are not your neighbor, your sister or your friends. You may have had experiences that are very similar to those experienced by other people, but they are not you, nor are you them. Your experiences are personal to you. They are your successes and they are your failures, which are based, in turn, upon your actions, inactions, reactions, memories and beliefs, not anyone else's. You cannot and should not be lumped together with anyone else. That would be like comparing apples and oranges; both from the same food group but completely different.

You are not like anyone else other than the fact that you come from the same species. To be treated the same, without taking into account your individual uniqueness, is to set you up for failure. You won't find that here. My intent is to see you succeed.

This book is designed to recognize what a wonderful individual you are and to celebrate your unique qualities. It is designed to use your individuality to your advantage. In this book we don't clone and we don't loan. We bring you home to realize the magnificence of your own.

So, if you are willing to accept that you are a marvelous and creative individual, if you are willing to accept that you are unique, capable and intelligent, we can get started with the process of teaching you how to realize that, not only do you have a path in life, not only can that path can lead you to creativity, fulfillment and success, but that you have all the say in what that path is, where it leads and how to go about clearing the brush to its discovery.

WARNING!!

The path upon which you are about to embark is not something to be taken lightly. As you go through this process you will be poked and prodded and pushed. You will learn things about yourself that may surprise you. The trick is to allow yourself these realizations so that you can move forward on your path to happiness and success.

If you allow yourself this gift, you will move forward with a confidence not previously known. You will, if you do the work, find understanding, direction and hope. You will find yourself. You will discover that, in the end, it really is all about "me."

> *"Everyone is a genius. But if you judge a fish*
> *on its ability to climb a tree, it will live its*
> *whole life believing that it is stupid."*
> - Albert Einstein

INTRODUCTION

So, what is the secret to success? Why do some people make it while others do not? Is there some magic formula or spell to be cast for someone to become the success that they want to become?

Let me assure you that there is no bewitching store from which to buy your success, no futuristic laboratory to hire for a change of DNA. There is no incantation hidden away in some ancient scroll buried deep inside a pyramid, and you don't have to look out into the wide expanse of the Universe to find it. No, the only travel destination you will need is the nearest mirror. There is a secret, and it is as plain as the nose on your face. The solution to finding this secret is that you have to be willing to look past your nose to the bigger reflection, and then past that one as well.

You are your secret to success. Yes, I know you have heard that before. Like many, however, you just chose not to believe it, or you didn't take it seriously enough to stop looking outside yourself for the answer. Well, let me take a minute to assure you that *you* are your starting point. Now that the secret is out, let's talk about how to make the best of you. (There is, after all, an order to things.)

As you will discover in the following pages, "starting from where you are" is always best. (Actually, it is the only place you can start.) But there is more to it than that. It is about seeing where you have been, the actions you have taken, the patterns you have developed, how your past has affected your present and how it will affect your future if you do nothing to understand it or change the pattern.

So, here you are, and this is a good place to start. If you are ready, turn the page and take the next step towards a happier, more creative and successful you.

CHAPTER 1

Understanding Where You Are

The first step towards realizing your success is two-fold: understanding where you are and how you got here. The second step is accepting responsibility for it.

Most people tend to focus on the unpleasant aspects of their past. You know, those experiences that cause us to cringe, cry, and hide. For some of us, however, it is not enough just to remember those experiences. Many of us tend to hyper-focus on the negative aspects of those experiences to the exclusion of all else. Those hurts and failures make us want to hide our heads, all the while hoping that no one else has noticed or will notice them. We allow those negative experiences to overshadow any good that we have done. Why?

Because these are our failures: They are what we think others remember of us. They are those same memories that are probably running rampant through your mind right now. They are the memories that keep us down and depressed, if we let them. They are the memories that we allow into our psyche as the prophet of our future.

Everyone has heard the voice of doom at some time or other:

"There is no use in trying. You will only fail again, so you might as well give up and be content where you are. It is safe to be here in your misery. It may not be what you want but it is what you know. Besides, it could be worse."

But even with this voice booming in our heads, we feel a need to do and have more. It is what everyone wants: to be more than they are, to live a better life, to be happy and successful: to feel fulfilled. Why, then, is it so difficult to move forward? Why does the past have so much power over us? This is why understanding where you are, (and who you are) is so critically important.

Everything you have ever said, thought or experienced has not only brought you to where you are, it has molded you into who and what you are. You are, in fact, a composite of your past: every person with whom you have ever interacted, every book you have read, every television program you have watched, every success you have experienced and every failure you have suffered.

From these life experiences you have formed opinions, feelings, morals and beliefs about yourself and the world around you. Even your experiences today, in the last five minutes and at this very moment have influence over you. Thus, you can probably understand why some believe that you are defined by your past.

> *But there is a difference between learning*
> *from the past and living from the past.*
> --Gerald Reiche

If you are your past, it is important to identify and understand those aspects of your past that have kept you from moving forward. Note the key word: "**understand**."

The word: "understand" is defined by Merriam-Webster as "to grasp the meaning of." It is *not* defined as looking at your past experiences and belittling yourself for making a particular choice or series of choices.

Yes, you are responsible for every choice you make, but just as there is a difference between living and learning from the past, there is also a difference between conscious and unconscious choice. We will discuss this more in the coming chapters. For now, it is enough to start with the proposition of being honest with yourself about your past and its effects on where and who you are today. The following exercise will help with your understanding of this concept.

EXERCISE 1: MY PAST

The purpose of this exercise is to get you reacquainted with yourself: who you are and where these ideas of yourself come from. Here you will remember some of your greatest influences, both positive and negative, where you developed your likes and dislikes, what caused you to make the changes that you have made and why you have not made the changes you would like to have made. This exercise will help you understand who you are, and help you see that ultimately, it is you that brought you here. This is the first step toward moving you onto your path of a more creative, fulfilling and successful life.

If you have thoughts of skipping over this exercise, please think again. As I have learned, knowing who you are, how you got here and how these choices brought you here is important to your future. It is where you start looking at the past in an objective manner so that you can learn from it rather than allowing yourself to fall into the trap: that of "living from that past." It will help you move forward to where you would really like to be.

Below are some opportunities to help you reconnect with you. The answers can be written in this book but it may be more helpful for you to use a separate notebook. Since we are all in a constant state of change you may have a desire to revisit these exercises at some point in the future.

Please be descriptive in your answers. For example, state who is with you, where you are, what you are doing. Describe the area around you. Describe how you feel about the event and the choices you made because of those feelings.

Example: My first memory takes place at about the age of three. I am at a playground with two girls. They are our neighbor's children. Their mother is watching us play. I am riding a tricycle. It is a warm, sunny day in Southern California. I am very happy riding the tricycle and being the center of attention.

There is a large chain link fence surrounding the playground. I am very familiar with this place as we have been here before. I am having a great deal of fun until it is time to leave. I want to stay but I know that making a fuss will only get me in trouble. So, although I am pouting, I choose not to say anything and leave as I am told.

Now it is time for you to write about your own first memory, memorable experience, and some other notable times of your life.

MY FIRST MEMORABLE
EXPERIENCE :-)

Here you are to write about the first experience (other than the very first memory) that comes to mind. The difference? Your first memory, in this context, is more of an observation than an activity where you interacted with others. Memory does not necessarily involve action on your part whereas experience does. It is your hands-on activity and the resulting interaction with others that is the subject of this first exercise. It does not matter if the experience was pleasurable or not. Just write about your first active experience.

MY FIRST DATE :-)

If you have not yet started dating, imagine what your first date would look like. With whom would you have your date? Where would you go? What would you do? How would it end? Otherwise write about your first date. Where did you go? Do you think it went well? What were your perceptions of your date's assessment of you? Why?

MY FIRST SUCCESS :-)

What was your first success? Where were you? What were you doing? Were you interacting with others or were you alone? How did you feel about it? How did the people around you react? (Either someone witnessed your success or they had an opportunity to listen to your excitement as you regaled them with your story.) Looking back, what do you think you learned about yourself in the experience?

MY FIRST FAILURE :-(

What happened? How did it make you feel? What did you do about it? Did you get up and try again or did you give up? What was your perception of how others around you reacted? How do you feel about it today?

MY LATEST SUCCESS :-)

How is this success the same or different than your first? Are your feelings and reactions the same? Different? What about your perceived reaction of others around you?

MY LATEST "FAILURE" :-(

How does this compare to the first? Are your feelings the same? Different? What about how you perceive the reactions of those around you?

COMMONALITIES

In this last part of this exercise, I want you to go through these questions and look for the commonalities. Mostly, identify your perceived reactions from others, thoughts of yourself and actions that you took as a result. List them here for future reference.

These few memories/events that I have asked you to revisit are not necessarily going to give you a complete picture of your feelings and emotions, nor are they necessarily going to create enough of a pattern to identify and understand all of the choices you have made in your life. There are many more experiences, perceptions, reactions and thought patterns making up your life. Some of them are probably already starting to buzz through your head. Using these as your starting point, however, you will begin to form an understanding about your history and how the choices from those events have landed you here. Yes, you are responsible for your choices but remember that this process is intended to help you to understand them, not to make you beat yourself up because of them.

I used the terms: "success" and "failure" for this first exercise because they bring about specific emotions. These emotions are universally similar but their meanings and effects are relative. They are unique to the individual defining them, which makes them relevant to that individual (you).

We have all heard sayings like: "One's best success comes after his (or her) greatest disappointments." We can also understand the statement that one person's failure might be another's success. What we are really talking about here is perception: that same perception or opinion that each of us has developed about ourselves over our lifetimes. It is through our own view of our past that we find the events that have formed our opinions of ourselves and our perceptions/opinions and outlook about the likelihood of our success in the future.

So, it is by looking at the events of our past that we find one of the best methods for determining where these outlooks and perceptions come from and how to go about changing them (and, consequently, ourselves) so that we can move in the direction we would like to go.

Here is an example of how looking at my own past has enabled me not only to change my perspective of a fairly significant event in my life, but which also taught me about reactive patterns, which allowed me to move forward on a better path. This example is not intended to be a comparison for anything that has or is going on in your life. Rather, it is intended to get you thinking about your own thought patterns and choices.

My first marriage lasted about eight years. The day it ended I was depressed and angry that I had wasted so much time in what was obviously a huge mistake. I was also having doubts about my value as a husband since I was a man, and men are supposed to fix things (pattern) but I was not able to fix this one. My perception about myself, and my perspective about life in general was that I was a failure and it was not going to get any better. I had allowed myself to become a single father, I had allowed my family to incur a great deal of debt and now I had to work two jobs to make ends meet. There was no light, no rainbow and it did not feel as though there was any hope.

My perspective changed, however, when I allowed myself to understand that I had an opportunity to love and be loved, even if it was for a very short time. That little bit of love brought a child, made me a father which taught me more about life, love and the human experience than I could ever have imagined. I would never have had this wonderful opportunity and, in all likelihood, would not have taken those actions which then led me to my second marriage (which I hold very dear) and a life for which I am now very grateful.

You see, I could have stayed in that life of depression and negativity and self-imposed misery, choosing to settle for so much less than I have now, or I could decide to change my perspective of my past, my present and the outlook for my future. It was my choice, no one else's.

Of course, this is my own perspective/outlook/opinion of what happened during that time of my life. Someone else experiencing the same things may have ended up with a completely different conclusion and may have chosen go in a completely different direction. Mine was to wake myself from that stupor of negativity and move forward. I stopped listening to that voice of doom and focus on more the positive aspects of my life. What I recognized was that I was listening to the same redirect that had caused me to stay in my misery in the first place. I knew this was not where I wanted to stay and so I put aside all of that fear-based self talk and allowed my perspective to change. No, it was not easy. The doubts were very persistent. But with each step I took it became more evident that I had found my path to a good place. I focused on taking one step at a time: Sometimes big steps, sometimes small. The point was to keep my feet moving. Before I knew it, I had moved beyond my past and into a much brighter future.

Perception, perspective, outlook, opinion; it does not really matter what one calls it. It is enough to know that it is personal to each of us, just like the past to which we tend to cling. Others may voice their agreement with your outlook but their experience is not your experience. They did not experience it. You did. Their perceptions and their opinions are based on a compilation of their own life experiences, which although seemingly similar to yours, are really very, very different.

Have you ever watched a movie that you thought was absolutely one of the best you had ever seen, yet someone else thought it boring and amateurish? Why do you think two very different opinions could arise from the same movie? Probably for the same reason that your taste in food is also so different. Does that make either of you right or wrong? Of course not! It just means that you have different tastes and opinions. Why? BECAUSE YOU ARE TWO COMPLETELY DIFFERENT INDIVIDUALS. It does not matter if you lived in the same house, went to the same schools and ate the same peanut butter and jelly sandwiches for lunch. You are different people with your own unique experiences resulting in your own unique feelings, challenges, likes and dislikes. Your thoughts are yours and theirs are theirs and the two shall never be anything else.

Have I emphasized this concept enough? It is absolutely necessary that you understand that you are unique and unparalleled in your individuality and that is the simple truth. But that is not your only truth, oh no! For you are so much more than that. You, because of your individual nature, have things to offer that no one else could. Your perceptions, because they are different than everyone else's, provide you with the ability to see things like no one else can. This unique insight allows you to mold your vision of yourself and others and your surroundings into something wonderfully and beautifully your own.

Think about this: Have you not already allowed yourself to see how things could be different if you were in charge? If not, see yourself in charge. Have you seen the differences you would have made in a piece of art or a movie or a garden, or how things are done where you work? Have you not already wondered why something so simple to your eye could be so difficult for someone else to see? It is a very interesting question to ponder, is it not?

One of my favorite sayings about what is happening to your mind, at this very moment, goes something like this:

> *"One's mind, once stretched by a new idea*
> *never regains its original dimensions."*
> --Oliver Wendell Holmes, Sr.

Let's stretch some more. Shall we?

CHAPTER 2

Dreams, Goals and Passions

*"What would you attempt if you
knew you could not fail?"*

--Robert H. Schuller

Everyone has dreams. Dreams feed and nurture our need for more. Many think that their purpose is to obtain more money, toys, travel and opportunity, but I firmly believe that this cannot be the extent of anyone's dreams. It's too narrowly focused. It does not take into account the extent of the word. I believe real purpose is found in the very simple truth that we can never stop growing, no matter where we are in life.

Regardless of how content we may be, how perfect things may appear, there is always a new lesson, a new thought, or a new way of seeing things. We cannot help but grow. Perhaps our purpose is to recognize this fact, embrace the change and grow into the better person that this realization brings about.

The bottom line is this: we are inquisitive, creative beings at our core. We think, we breathe, we create. We create to experience and that experience brings about the desire for more, and so we think again, breathe in new life, create a new experience. It is a continuous cycle, which we repeat over and over again: Think, breathe, create, experience. That is the essence of our human existence. It is what we do each and every second of our lives. We cannot stop it, nor can we live without it. When we try to curtail it (and many of us do) our attempts only increase that desire which, ultimately, results in a new experience in spite of our attempts to interfere. The result may not be what we would like to have experienced in the first place, but we experience the change nonetheless. In other words, our experience does not stop. It merely changes the experience we would have had because of our own interference with our natural desire to experience greater.

The universe is full of change and that change comes about because of the need to create, and creation begins with a single thought. Your unique ability to apply your thoughts to whatever circumstance presents its self is what determines the outcome of that creation.

You need to understand that you have a profound effect on everything that happens in your life. The effect that you have is based upon your thoughts about yourself. The thoughts you have about yourself are based on your perspective of your past. They are based upon how others react, what they say, (or rather, what you think they are saying) and your ability to recognize that all of this has absolutely nothing to do with whether you choose to step onto that path that leads to your good. You see, it is up to you to decide whether you will stay trapped in your past, continuing to listen to that naysayer that has kept you stagnant for so long. It is your choice, your responsibility, and your life.

If this makes sense and you are ready to do something about making your dream a reality, then it is time to take another step forward.

This step deals with you and only you. It focuses on your likes and your dislikes. It allows you to recognize those unique aspects of you and onto what path they might lead.

Identifying Your Passion

I am going to break into this part of the conversation/exercise and spend a moment with those of you who are not yet clear on your life's passion.

It is easy to sit here and say that everyone has a passion, but a large part of the reason many of us are unhappy with where we are is because we thought we knew what we wanted to do for the rest of our lives but, when we actually started doing it, found that it was not what we had envisioned after all. (Affectionately called the "this ain't it" syndrome.)

Understand that there is nothing wrong with you or the place you have found yourself. People experience "this ain't it" all the time. So, it is not wrong or unusual to try something, decide, "this ain't it" and then try something else. We do it all the time with our tastes in food, music, movies, friends, clothing, cars, vacations, and pretty much everything else in life. Why should a life's activity be any different?

The point is to realize that, when "this ain't it," it is okay to try something else. We only get a short time in this life and being able to live it from a place of fun and excitement and passion is important.

No one can live our lives for us. No one else can tell us what we should or will be passionate about. How miserable a life that would be! It is up to us to decide where we are the happiest. Who else but us would know what makes us happy? What a boring existence it would be if we had to pick something and stick with it no matter how distasteful we found it to be!

So, let us take a look at some things that will help you figure out the kinds of stuff that will fill your sails. Be patient with yourself. This may take a little thought and maybe some time. But it will be worth it in the end.

We will start with a basic, reflective exercise of writing down the kinds of things you do well on the page following this discussion (or in your notebook). Include your positive traits. Those are the things that you like about yourself, what others have told you they like about you, etc. For example: do you like to speak in public? Do you like to help others solve problems? Are you athletic? Do you like to read? Write? Teach?

What do people notice about you? Why do they come to you for help? What were (or are) your favorite subjects in school? What are the favorite aspects of your work? The people? The customers? What do you get out of it besides a paycheck?

Now make a list of those positive traits you see in yourself and add in the answers to the above questions. I'll start the list with the traits that I already know are true for you.

Take some time to mull all of this over and add as much as you think appropriate to the list. We both know you have many more positive traits than just these few. The list will start on the next page.

My List of Positives

These are the traits that I know are true about you.
(I have written them in the first person for you to copy onto your list.)

I am intelligent

I am capable

I am creative

I am intuitive

I am a self-starter

I am compassionate

I am outgoing

I matter

I am well liked

I am valued

I am enough

Add to your list by asking yourself questions like these:

People come to me for advice about:

My favorite activities are:

Things I like about myself:

People tell me I am good at:

My favorite subjects in school were/are:

Now that you have a list (not necessarily a complete list because you are going to continue to discover more and more about yourself as you move forward in your quest) of your traits, likes and so forth, take a minute to read it over in a quiet place and then close your eyes, take a few deep breaths to relax yourself, and let all of the good you just listed sink in. Then, when you are ready, (you'll know) take a long, deep cleansing breath and allow your mind to clear.

When all of the distractions have gone, when you are relaxed, allow yourself to answer the following question: "*What would I attempt if I knew that I could not fail?*" (Id)

The answer may be instantaneous or it may take a few minutes before something comes to you. When it does come, write it down as one of your three passions or dreams. Does it matter whether this ends up being what you decide to do for the rest of your life? Not hardly, but it is a starting point.

This exercise is intended to give you some tools to help you get moving in the right direction. If this exercise did not also lead you to thoughts of other things you have always wanted to do, you may want to repeat the exercise. If you cannot seem to get past the one thought, don't worry. One is all you really need. After all, one can only have one thought and take one action at a time. (I know I will get cards and letters and e-mails from all of you multi-taskers, and that's okay too.)

Remember, inaction gets you nowhere. Action, even if it turns out to be something other than your ultimate goal, is a start.

As Will Rogers once said: "Even if you're on the right track, you'll get run over if you just sit there."

In keeping with the idea of movement, let's move on to another exercise.

Exercise #2: My Dreams

"Ask yourself what makes you come alive,
and go do that, because what the world
needs is people who have come alive."

--Howard Thurman

On the following page (or in your notebook) I want you to write three goals or dreams or passions that you have always had but, for one reason or another, have never pursued. (This should include what popped into your mind in the previous exercise.) These three dreams do not need to appear in any particular order, nor does it matter how they compare to anyone else's list. There are no right or wrong answers. These are your dreams and yours alone. Whether you just figured it out or only have an inkling about it, write what you think it is. Remember, the only constant in this world is change, which means that it is okay to change your mind.

Some examples might be:
Write a book
Earn a degree in math
Move to New England
Run a marathon
Drive a bus
Build a house
Become a teacher
Captain a cruise ship
Go to medical school

Get the idea? Good. Now turn the page or grab your notebook and write. Again, do not be embarrassed, self-conscious or worried that they are different (or the same) as someone else's dreams. It also doesn't matter if they are not what someone else would choose for you to do. These are **your** dreams, not theirs.

In my opinion, no one should ever be stuck doing what he or she does not want to do. As you know from my own biography, I have gone through my share of "this ain't its" and there is nothing wrong with that. Especially if it ultimately gets you the "this is it" you want to be.

Face it: if everyone were to be stuck where they land, Edison would have stopped long before that 2000th attempt at the light bulb. The point is to move forward toward a happier, more creative, more fulfilling life. If it turns out to be something different, at least you can say you did not spend a lifetime getting run over by a train.

There is an old story, the origin of which is somewhat unclear. It is about a man who walked the same route to work every day. One day he fell into a hole. The next day, walking the same route, he came upon the same hole and fell in again. The third day, tired of falling into the hole, he decided to walk in a different direction. Aren't you tired of falling into that hole? Perhaps you should walk in a different direction as well.

The reason I am asking you to list three dreams is to allow choice but also to force you to focus and avoid the risk of becoming overwhelmed. Many people, if their list is too long and involved, tend not to know which way to turn. They become frustrated and lost and give up. The idea is to avoid situations that cause you to give up. Therefore, we limit our focus so that we can move in the direction we want to move: toward a happier, more creative and fulfilling life.

Okay, so now it is time to get back on track to the original exercise. So turn the page (or grab your notebook) and write. For those of you who have more than three dreams or goals, choose the three that speak to you the most, meaning those in which you have the most interest. What if you have more than three and you cannot decide which three are more compelling that the others? Just pick three. It will not matter which of the three you choose for this exercise.

If you only have two, don't worry about the third. If you know the one thing that you want to do in life more than anything else, write it down and don't worry about the other two. This exercise, and your life are not defined by the number of dreams you have at this moment, or at any other moment for that matter. There are many more important things about you that define who you are. You will, no doubt, discover more of them as you continue on your path.

My Three Dreams

1.

2.

3.

How does that feel: to have your dreams down on paper? Excited about getting started? Hesitant and/or anxious about whether you can do it? Do you hear the chatter from that "Doubting Thomas" coming from the back of your head? You know, that voice that always tries to tell you that you can't?

Let's talk about that "you can't" part a little more. The next couple of pages fall under the title: "My Top Ten Excuses." On these pages (or in your notebook) I want you to write one of your dreams and then, under that dream, list the first ten excuses that come to mind for not having gone after your dream before and/or the reasons why you are having doubts about it now. Although I am sure that your mind is full of them, I'll provide the following example to get you started.

DREAM: Run a marathon

EXCUSES: I'm too old
I don't have the time to train
I can't run
I don't have the energy
I can't afford the running shoes
I need to lose some weight first
I can't afford the entry fee
I'm not that athletic
I have too many other things on my plate
I don't know how to train for a marathon

Once you are finished with the excuses for the first dream, do the same for the second and then the third.

My Top Ten Excuses

Dream:

Excuses:

1.

2.

3.

4.

5.

6.

7.

8.

9.

10.

Dream:

Excuses:

1.

2.

3.

4.

5.

6.

7.

8.

9.

10.

Dream:

Excuses:

1.

2.

3.

4.

5.

6.

7.

8.

9.

10.

By the time you have finished this "excuse" exercise, you will probably have started noticing a pattern. (In this case, it is probably the same kinds of excuses showing up over and over again about why you cannot pursue your dream/passion.)

It is not really all that surprising that many of the same excuses show up for your three different dreams or passions. The Ego or "Doubting Thomas" seldom has its own, original ideas. Why should it? The same doubts and fears have worked very well this far. Why fix it if it ain't broke, right?

But this is so very much different from your creative side! Your creative self taps into an ever-widening stream of ideas and possibilities. Remember how you used to get all excited when you came up with a new and innovative way of doing something? The possibilities seemed endless! That is because the possibilities <u>are</u> endless! So what happened? Ego started to get in the way, soaking up your creative juices like a sponge soaks up a spill: casting doubt and, eventually, stalling out your engine. That is where your excuse list came from. Now let's take a look at the root cause.

CHAPTER 3

Fear of Failure and Lack of Self Worth

F ear is a natural instinct. It comes from a need for self-preservation: the "fight, flight or freeze" reaction to a perceived danger. In the "old days" there might have been a vicious beast waiting to devour you beyond that next tree or rock or just outside of the cave. Fortunately, for most of us this is no longer a concern. But the modern world does have its own version of the beast: slow economics, high jobless rates, bigger demands in the workplace, the cost of education, crowded schools, family needs and the list goes on. Is there any wonder that people are afraid of failure? The consequences can be enormous!

And yet, there is a natural desire for more: more money, better jobs, more toys and so on. In addition to all of this, is that natural urge that goes beyond the "keeping up with the Joneses" mentality. There is an urge to expand one's self to be better than we are today. There is a desire to experience more: to grow internally as a person, to become that expression of life we picture ourselves to be. It is in this desire to grow where many get stuck.

We all want more which tends to make us want to improve ourselves. But this requires our doing something about it. You know, taking chances. But, when we think about taking those chances necessary for growth, we become fearful of failing, which then keeps us from taking those chances, which then leads to that guilty feeling for not taking those chances, which makes us want to do something about it, and so on. What a vicious circle! But wait...there's more!

That guilty feeling, caused by our not having taken the chances that we were so afraid of taking, turns on us. It casts doubt about our ability to improve our lives, which then leads right back into that circle of fear and doubt and shame from which we started. It can bring about a feeling of self-loathing or lack of self-worth, which many of us know as that "not good enough" syndrome. And you thought you were alone in this cycle. No, my friend, you are not alone. Many (too many) of us have landed here and many more will follow.

Fortunately, it does not need to be this way. There is a way out of the cycle. Your way out is to continue working through this book and reach for that brass ring you have allowed to elude you...up until now.

Look. Everyone is different. We all have our own likes and dislikes, our own loves and yearnings and fears. Life could not be any other way. We are all uniquely different (thank God) but we are also very much the same. We all have the same general fears and the same general hopes and desires. The only difference is that some of us have been able to move forward with our dreams while others of us just need a little push and/or reassurance. Do you think successful people worry about whether someone will like their book or their music or their product or service? Of course they do! Their path is no different than yours. They just started a little earlier or caught on a little more quickly. Does that matter? No. Why? Because that is *their* path and not yours. Your path started when you picked up this book.

Remember: The first step on your path is the realization that you start from where you are.

The second is accepting responsibility for your life.

The third step is allowing yourself to acknowledge that you are capable, intelligent (if not brilliant), creative and unique, and entitled to move your life in the direction that you choose. I think Marianne Williamson said it best:

> *"Our deepest fear is not that we are inadequate.*
> *Our deepest fear is that we are powerful beyond*
> *measure. It is our light, not our darkness that*
> *most frightens us. We ask ourselves, who am I to*
> *be brilliant, gorgeous, talented and fabulous?*
> *Actually, who are you not to be? You are a child of*
> *God. Your playing small does not serve the world.*
> *There's nothing enlightened about shrinking so*
> *that other people won't feel insecure around you.*
> *We were born to make manifest the glory of God*
> *that is within us. Its not just in some of us; it's in*
> *everyone. And as we let our own light shine, we*
> *unconsciously give other people permission to do*
> *the same. As we are liberated from our own fear,*
> *our presence automatically liberates others."*

Remember, You Start From Where You Are

So, where are you now? Hopefully you are in a place where you can understand that you are a magnificently unique individual with a life that rivals that of any other person on earth. You know your past, your doubts and your fears. You have a clue about your passion and what has kept you from moving forward to enjoy an even happier and more creative, fulfilling and successful life than you have ever experienced.

You know that everyone has the same basic wants and needs, and that everyone has that natural desire to create, grow and experience more in life. You can understand your fears and you know that, to be *living* from your past is suicidal whereas *learning* from your past can be quite helpful in moving forward with your future.

So, where do you go from here? It would be prudent to continue identifying, understanding and dealing with the obstacles to your success. The next section will delve into that in more detail.

Ego: The Voice of Reason? Or the Voice of Fear!

Intellectually we all understand how we have allowed ourselves to get caught up in the past. Just thinking of all those years that we kept ourselves trapped by our failures and disappointments is probably enough to do it. But how could we allow the past to have so much control? We think about all of those mistakes in judgment, all of those disapproving faces, all of those people doing the "I told you so" dance when our dreams failed. Consequently we tend to start believing that success is not in the cards. Well, not in *our* cards anyway. That thought process often goes something like this:

"What a waste of time! How could I have embarrassed myself like that? They told me it would not work; that my dreams were impossible. Obviously they know more than I know about this. Maybe what I want to do really is impossible. Or, maybe I'm just not good enough!"

See how easy it is to step into the trap? Do you see all of the generalities in that self-condemnation? Do you see all of the assumptions made? It is so easy to point to ourselves and instead of understanding the real reason the idea did not work, allowing it to become the mantra of our life.

Before you go any further, I want to repeat something that you already know, and I want you to write it down somewhere that you will see it often. It needs to be repeated and repeated to help overcome that self-defeating attitude that you are so used to falling into. It is something that, no matter what anyone says, and regardless of your past, you know deep within the recesses of your soul to be the absolute truth. You just need to allow the words to be heard:

"I am worthy. I am smart. I am capable. I am talented. I am as entitled to success and fulfillment as anyone who has ever come before me. I matter. I am enough."

Think about it. If this were not your truth, you would never experience hope or get up to try again. The problem does not lie with your brains or your abilities but with the convincing voice of your Ego. It is an all too familiar voice to which we all fall victim at one time or another.

So how do we deal with this Ego thing? Can we get rid of it? Sorry, it is not something that can be thrown away or discarded or even removed through surgery. It is part of who we are. But what we *can* do is to learn to recognize Ego's voice, its purpose and its effect. Then, just like the guy who fell into the hole, we can learn to take a different path and avoid Ego's hole entirely. We can learn to think critically.

Critical Thinking

The term: "Ego" seems to have morphed over the years from the originally intended reference to the "I" or self of any person. Nowadays it seems to connote a derogatory form of placing or thinking of one's self as being above or better or beyond others. The modern term seems to have more to do with conceit or self-absorption (egotism) as opposed to recognizing the uniqueness of one's self. There is after all, a difference.

We have all said or thought it: "Wow! What an Ego!" Correct? Well, in our use of the term, we are less concerned with this reference to the anti-social, self- absorbed aspect of the "egocentric" personality. What we are focused on is the lesser known psychoanalytical characteristic of the self, which is defined by Dictionary.com as follows: "The part of the psychic apparatus that experiences and reacts to the outside world and thus mediates between the primitive drives of the Id (Ego for our purposes) and the demands of the social and physical environment." *(Editorial added)*

In other words, that part of us which experiences not only our own reaction to a given situation, but which also tends to notice how everyone else is reacting and what everyone else is saying. We are looking at what we hear (or perceive), everyone else seems to be saying about us as truth.

Remember, Ego comes from our instinct for survival. It is our reaction to things with which we find discomfort. It is the heart beating faster when we know something scary is about to happen (or when we perceive someone's fear). It is the heightened sense of awareness we experience when we walk down a dark alley. It is our reaction when faced with our worse nightmares: speaking in public, jumping from a perfectly good airplane or any number of events that make us uncomfortable. It can also be our reaction to someone else's fear of these same things.

Whatever the event, we all recognize the voice and the effect it can have upon us, and those around us. The difference, after having pointed it out, is that once identified, we can learn to apply listening skills and alternative behavioral skills that will allow us to move beyond the walls Ego has built between each of us and our dreams. We call this "critical thinking."

If we look at Ego realistically, we see it as a natural warning mechanism. It's kind of like turning on the hazard lights of a car when there is an emergency. The difference is that Ego works *without* our consciously turning on the switch. Left to run rampant, Ego becomes an insurmountable obstacle to forward movement: a saboteur intent on causing failure and returning us to the safety of the familiar. It works on us with reminders of the past and hints that we are about to embark on some new unknown that will surely end in disaster.

As harsh as it can be, Ego is not really our enemy. When we realize Ego's purpose, its nagging voice of doubt becomes a helpful tool we use to *learn* from our past mistakes rather than allowing ourselves to be bound by those mistakes. Understanding Ego's natural function allows us to recognize its value as a counterbalance to impulsivity. The key is to achieve balance between the two. Of course, that does not mean that we are immune from Ego's ever-ongoing attempts to regain control. None of us are. Not even the most successful of us! Let me give you an example of what I am talking about.

I once attended a seminar hosted by a multiple, best-selling author. During the course of the seminar, the issue of self-doubt (Ego) came up. Now, understand that this is a world acclaimed author who has appeared in nationally televised talk shows, spoken to sold-out crowds and who has experienced the kind of success of which many dreams are made. Yet with all of this success, this person continued to deal with the trickery of Ego which suggested that she really was *not* cut out to be a writer; that she had no talent and that her past successes were just flukes. Fortunately, this individual was able to recognize Ego's voice, analyze what she was hearing and move forward with her next best seller. She was able to take a step back, look at it objectively and move on. She used her critical thinking skills, just as you will.

It seems strange, somehow, to talk about someone hugely successful as falling victim to the same Ego-based fears and doubts as the rest of us. It almost seems oxymoronic, does it not? And yet we constantly hear news stories of addiction and recovery, phobia and the return from anonymity. We critique performances, hire and fire based on our support or protest of their art. What we sometimes fail to realize in the glare of their spotlight is that these are people like us with their own likes and dislikes, dreams and excuses. I suppose the point here is that there is little difference between taking action to overcome what appears to be adversity and making your dreams reality. In both cases, we are heeding the call of a happier, more creative and fulfilling life.

So now it is time to take a look at your excuse list. Do you see those "insurmountable" reasons in a different light? Do you recognize the voice of Ego? Can you stop and analyze what you have written in a critical manner and realize that you are not too old or too poor, that you do have the ability to figure out your next step to making your dreams a reality? Of course you can.

Just remember this word of warning. Ego is not going to give up its lifetime of control over you willingly. It is and always will be there, lurking, waiting for the smallest hesitation; watching for that ounce of doubt to jump in and confirm your worst fears as true. You will likely stumble, even with the knowledge that the words coming from that position of doubt are just Ego's familiar words of fear, and that's okay. The difference, now, is that you have a tool with which to understand that this all comes from your fear-based self. It comes from your memories (perceptions) of past actions as failures. As you move forward with your work, you will discover that you have other tools to use in dealing with this naysayer as well. You may also realize that you are not the only one who has or will experience the dark side. Everyone does at one time or another. The point is that you are not alone. Although you are magnificently unique, that uniqueness does not keep you from the commonality of Ego's stare. It does, however, give you the ability to deal with Ego on your own terms.

Up until now we have been talking about helping you take steps on your path to creativity, fulfillment and success. Now let's take it one step further (pun intended) by helping you to see your path.

CHAPTER 4

Meditation, Visualization and Journaling

Now that you have identified that meddling voice called Ego, let me ask you this. Do you know what your dream looks like? Have you ever sat or walked in a quiet place and allowed yourself to dream of your success? Have you lost yourself in the vision of that wonderful reality that has always seemed just outside your grasp? Have you sat and contemplated what you would do once you arrive at that place? Have you taken pen to paper and jotted down your visions of what, when, where and how?

There are tools that you can use to help deepen your resolve for the pursuit of your passion. These tools allow you to see what it would be like to engage in that activity you seek. These tools allow you to experience the success that you would like to see while hinting at the direction you should be taking to get there. Let's take a look at the first of these tools: meditation.

Meditation

I know: just the word conjures up a whole host of images. Stereotypically, these images might include such things as the wrinkled old wise man sitting on a blanket, in a cave, next to his lone candle somewhere at the top of a mountain. On the other hand, it might be someone quietly getting lost in the moment while strolling along a sandy beach at sunset. Or it could even be someone listening to the enchanting echo of a meditation bowl in a quiet sanctuary.

There are an endless number of meditation scenarios that can and are practiced, and which are found around the world. According to Wikipedia, meditation refers to any of a family of practices in which the practitioner trains his or her mind, or self-induces a mode of consciousness in order to realize some benefit. Fancy words to describe getting lost in a daydream, but true nevertheless.

Whether visiting a bookstore, or searching for the definition of the term on-line, one can be overrun by the myriad of practices, choices, types, instructors and histories of meditation. One can find information on traditional or quiet meditation, transcendental meditation, the "being in the now" meditation, an altered state of consciousness meditation, guided meditation, silent meditation, walking meditation and well, you get the picture. But whatever it is called or how it is practiced, the common thread is the chance to clear the noise, to quiet the mind and to allow the river of creative juices to escape the confines of doubt and flow into our lives.

Most of us have, at one time or another, sought out the solitude. You know, that moment away from the busy-ness of life where one can relax and calm the self from the inside out. Whether you realized it at the time, you were more than likely engaging in some form of meditation.

Meditation is generally practiced either in the silence or with some soft, mellow, melodic sound in the background. Many use music, others use the sounds of the waves or the rain or a babbling brook. Some use a chant to help them focus. Some use a breathing technique like the one you practiced earlier. It can be done through the focus of a single sound, or by focusing on rise and fall of the chest as the air enters and leaves the body. It can be through the feeling of the heart beating in every corner of the body. There is no right or wrong way to meditate so long as it allows us to free our minds from the distractions of the day, and to open to that inward reflection of our truth.

A word of warning is appropriate here. Meditation is a very powerful tool and should not be done while driving or during any activity where not paying attention to what you are doing might lead to harm to either yourself or someone else. This applies equally to visualization and journaling. (I know this seems obvious but then so are the dangers of talking on the phone or texting while driving and yet how many people do you see engaging in those activities on a daily basis?)

Remember earlier when you were asked to close your eyes, breathe deeply and answer what you would do if you knew you could not fail? That was a form of meditation. You opened yourself to the endless possibilities of life and an answer presented its self to you. If you did not get an answer to your question, it is probably because you allowed distractions to invade your thoughts. In that case, where distracting thoughts invade, it is a matter of learning to quiet your mind. Or perhaps you tried too hard. In meditation, simply close your eyes, breathe deeply and allow the answer to come. You don't want to be so intent on expecting an answer that you are unable to recognize it when it does appear.

Like all things worthwhile, meditation takes practice. There are years of thoughts that you have allowed to race through your mind and it is sometimes difficult to suddenly shift to quiet contemplation. So, when you first begin, start from a place of understanding that Ego is the warning system against change. You should also understand that, if you are not used to the quiet, other things might tend to interrupt. These can be everyday things like the hum of the washing machine or the barking of the neighbor's dog or even the ticking of the clock on the wall. It does get easier though, and I encourage you to continue your efforts in whatever method comes most naturally. You may also want to try it in conjunction with visualization and journaling. Why don't we do a meditation exercise and see how it goes.

Meditation Exercise

For this exercise you will need a quiet place, free from distraction. You will need something with which to write and either your notebook or the next blank page in this book. I would recommend using that notebook you have been using all along, as it is sometimes difficult to fit the flood of ideas and information that come to you in the limited space that this book allows. There is no specific assignment for writing but it is often helpful to be able to jot down experiences or thoughts or realizations that come from this practice of engaging a peaceful mind. It is not intended to be a visualization exercise (which we will engage in later) Nevertheless, quieting the mind can result in a flood of ideas that have been waiting to burst into life. It never hurts to be prepared.

This exercise is hard to do at the same time that you are reading the directions, so it would be a good idea to read over the next several paragraphs before starting your meditation exercise until you are comfortable with the process. If you like, you can record it to play back, or you can have someone read it to you. There are no limits to the possibilities of how to practice meditation, as long as it works for you. Likewise, there are no limits to the benefits that will result.

The location for this exercise is not anywhere specific. It can be in your bedroom or on your living room couch. It can be in your backyard or in the local park. The location does not matter as long as you can have some quiet and are away from distraction. As we discussed earlier, there are already more than enough distractions running through your mind.

You may also want to use a timer or alarm if you have any limitation of time for this exercise. While most beginners find it difficult to stay in meditation for very long, occasionally someone will find that they lose track of everything but the openness of their mind, and that time has slipped away. It will also alleviate the tendency to keep checking to see how much time has been spent or that is left for the exercise rather than remaining focused on the movement of air and the rise and fall of the chest.

Once you find your place, get into a comfortable, seated position and set the clock. It may also be helpful to tape yourself (or someone else) reading the following several paragraphs to play back for your meditation, at least until you have the directions down:

GUIDED MEDITATION

Sit up straight but relaxed and close your eyes. Take in a long, deep breath through your nose, hold it for a second or two and let it out either through your nose, mouth or both. (If you have a cold or other cause that prohibits the use of your nose, just use your mouth.)

Feel the tension in your body leave as you exhale. Take another deep breath, hold it and let it out, again focusing on how easily the muscles of your body relax as you exhale. Do this one more time and notice the difference in yourself now, compared to when you started. You should feel relaxed and calm. (If you are one of those really nervous, tight-muscled people like me, you may need to repeat this once or twice more.)

Keeping your eyes closed, breathe normally and focus on the air as it enters and exits your body. Notice the rise and fall of your chest as the air moves in and out. (Do this for a few minutes.) If you find that you have random thoughts floating into your mind, acknowledge them and let them go while returning to the focus of the rise and fall of your chest. Stay focused on the rise and fall of your chest and allow yourself to stay open. You will know when to regain your awareness of your surroundings from your timer.

Stay open? To what? What exactly does that mean, you ask? For now I will give you a very general answer.

The Universe contains endless possibilities for your future. While you are the one behind the wheel, thereby making it your responsibility to steer your life, the act of opening your mind to the endless ideas and possibilities and directions will allow you to feel the direction of the wind (river if you prefer). The whole purpose is to allow you to experience the noiseless inspiration of what is possible.

It is very easy to allow one's self to become used to the noise and general busy-ness that is ever present in our lives. Between the television, the radio, Internet, car noise, traffic, crowds and so forth, we become conditioned to distraction. Ego knows this and uses it to its advantage against the change that quiet represents. But now you know about it, and perhaps this will help you to allow your intuition to come forward and your Ego to be quiet.

Perhaps it would be helpful to use an analogy I have heard used by Esther Hicks:

> *"It is more difficult to try and row upstream*
> *than to allow the river to carry you to your*
> *destination. The river is much more cooperative*
> *with the rudder's use as a directional when*
> *the boat is pointed down stream."*
>
> --Abraham-Hicks Publications

The point here is to stop fighting the uphill battle of life's distractions when there is a navigable path to help us get to our destination without running into the rocks. We can either go with the flow or stay stagnant against it.

As I said, there are many ways to meditate. Some use quiet, soothing music as a background, which I sometimes find beneficial. Some use a practice of keeping their eyes open and focusing on a point some ten feet or so in front of them. There are walking meditations and seated meditations. Some find running helps clear their minds of the many distractions of daily life. Yoga is another example of meditation and there are many, many others. It is important that you find what is right for you as a regular practice to allow your mind to clear away the distractions, and to allow you to open up to those endless possibilities that we talked about earlier.

When you have finished the quiet enjoyment of meditation, when you have allowed yourself to be open to the possibilities, we will move forward with the next part of the exercise: visualization.

Visualization

Visualization is a very widely used technique for realizing success. It gives the user something almost concrete to reach for. Athletes, and many others, use it in preparation for their events. Just watch the next weight lifter, high jumper, pitcher, quarterback, or entertainer as they prepare for their moment. Sometimes it is subtle, sometimes it is more pronounced. Nevertheless, it is there.

Visualization is used in all walks of life. The architect sees his or her structure standing magnificently, every detail accentuated by the skyline. Chess players see the outcome of their strategy ahead of their opponent's moves. Inventors see their ideas molded into reality and entrepreneurs listen to their intuition, envisioning their success before taking their next step. Let me give you an example.

Various studies have been conducted on the effects of visualization in sports. One example is a "basketball experiment" conducted by Professor L. V. Clark of Wayne State University in the 1960's.

Professor Clark studied two groups of high school basketball players over a two week period: those who practiced by shooting free-throws each morning and those who engaged in "mental practice," visualizing making shots but not actually doing real practice.

In basketball, free throws or foul shots are unopposed attempts to score points from a restricted area on the court and are generally awarded after a foul on the shooter by the opposing team.

Each successful free throw is worth one point. As you can imagine (no pun intended), a point based upon an unopposed shot can make a big difference in a game. It can also place a great deal of pressure on the shooter which often results in a lower scoring average than if the shot were being defended by an opposing player. Getting back to the study, here is how it went:

Prior to observation, both groups were tested on their free throw abilities and the results were recorded. At the conclusion of two weeks, both groups were tested again. The results were impressive! Both groups actually improved their free throw abilities a significant, measurable amount! (Clark LV. Effect of mental practice on the development of a certain motor skill. *Research Quarterly*, v31 n4 (Dec 1960):560-569.)

If you were to visualize your success, what would it look like? Is it pleasing to your senses? Does it take place in any specific area or genre? Can you see yourself doing it? How often do you think about achieving your dreams, seeing yourself as or doing whatever it is that you have always wanted to do? Do you find it hard not to think about success or about living a better life? Do you allow yourself such dreams, or do you allow Ego to keep such thoughts out?

Visualization comes naturally to all of us. It is a thought process, which leads to ideas, which lead to plans and actions and the real-life manifestation of thought. Thinking is the one thing that we all do, all day every day for as long as we are alive. We cannot help ourselves. It is what we do. Now, I know that some of us are sometimes accused of not thinking, even of being thoughtless, mindless or down right brainless. But in reality, nothing can be done, not done or undone without some thought process preceding the act (or inaction). We think, we dream, we take action to bring it into being. Of course the opposite is also true, for if we do not take action, the thought/dream does not manifest. Instead, the dream remains only a dream.

So, let us go back to that initial question: What does your dream look like? What does it sound like? How does it feel to the touch? How does your success make you feel? Do you become excited, relaxed, accomplished? Where does your dream take place? Who is with you? What things do you use to make it happen?

Most people have a general idea of what success means to them. Generally this includes wanting more, wanting to be happy, not wanting to worry about where the next meal is coming from, and so on. But that general idea of happiness or success is often where the thought process ends. Rarely do people take time to really sit down and think about their definition of happiness, fulfillment or success. For example, a very common desire is to meet "the right person." When asked what that means, one is generally the recipient of the following definition: "You know, someone nice."

While there is certainly nothing wrong with wanting "someone nice", I do not believe there to be a clearly defined persona here. Yes, there are a lot of "nice" people out there but does that mean their specific personality traits, habits, desires or views of life are going to match someone else's idea of the same? They really are not well stated in the term "someone nice".

As an example, I know a woman who, after her fair share of "nice guys" decided to take a different approach to her search for this ideal. (She took a different path in order to avoid falling into the pit of the redundant date.) She contemplated (meditated on) what traits she wanted in her mate, visualized the things she enjoyed in life and then made a list of those traits that matched her ideals. When she finished, she folded the list and put it in her purse where she could pull it out and re-examine the list whenever she wanted. In doing this, she set an intention of meeting that "right person" and then kept her eyes open for him to appear in her life. Did it work? What do you think?

Of course, there is more to it than making a list. Like anything else worthy of one's desire, it has to be thought about, mulled over, *meditated* upon and pulled from the intuitive part of us that knows the answer. Unfortunately, most tend not to listen to that intuitive voice. Rather, we give in to the doubts instilled by the Ego's attempts to maintain the status quo.

How do we know the difference between Ego and intuition? Think about what is attached to each. Do you feel excitement (intuition) or apprehension (Ego)? Do you feel calm assurance (intuition) or fear (Ego)? Do you feel hope (intuition) or a sense of doom (Ego)? That it is the right thing to do (intuition)?

Let's do another exercise to emphasize the point.

So, now it is time to take out that notebook again and write a list of those traits or qualities that are important for your perfect guy or girl. If you already have a wonderful significant other, do it anyway and see how all of those things you cherish in that person match up to your list. Understand that these qualities are the really important things. They are the deal-breakers. Yes, everyone is going to have some habit or quirk that you may think slightly annoying (or very annoying). But, that minor something is far outweighed by those traits that you consider really, really crucial in a relationship. So, think long and hard about your list and do not be surprised if you change it a few times as you re-read it.

Here is a portion of the list my wife made about a year before we met. (That would be the person I referred to earlier).

My Ideal Person:

Intelligent

Sense of humor

Spiritual

Wants children

Warm

Loving

Tall

Willing to leave California

Career oriented

Hard working

Handy around the house

Enjoys the arts/music/theater

Get the idea? Good. Now it is your turn. Feel free to use some or all of these on the list my wife wrote. I am sure you will have others of your own.

Visualization Exercise

In this exercise you will need a couple of things. One is to have a focus question. The other is to have a quiet place, a pad of paper and writing utensil for jotting down your notes. To make it easy I am going to feed you the focus question as follows:

"What would I attempt if failure were not an option?"

To get started, find a comfortable, quiet place to sit. Get in a comfortable position, take in a deep breath through your nose and then exhale it through your nose, mouth or both. Do this twice more. You will start to feel a relaxation in your body: a lessening of the tenseness, a lifting of the stress.

Now, you can focus on the question before you: *What would I attempt if failure were not an option?* Jot down what comes to you in your notebook. Do not concern yourself with whether what comes to you seems plausible or possible. Just write it down. Much like a brain storming session, there are no right or wrong answers, only ideas and information. You may find a common theme among the things you write down, or not. Either way, just write.

Do not be surprised if you have a very strong and vivid picture form in your mind of you doing what you write. If you do, allow it to come. Relax into it and see where it takes you.

You might be thinking that this exercise seems an awful lot like meditation. While there are some similarities, it is important to be able to tell the difference. Both require a quiet place and focus, but that is about where the similarities end.

Meditation is a process where the mind and body are relaxed and cleared of thought so that one can allow in and experience their true self without the interjections of Ego. Visualization, on the other hand, involves a specific thought or idea upon which to obtain a specific result. It is much like the athlete seeing the perfection of motion before going through with that motion.

Now that you have had a taste of both, I hope you can see how they can be applied to anything and everything in life, from the perfect mate to the perfect job, to the perfect house, to the creation of a fulfilling, more creative and successful life. Now we will add to your fund of success by turning our attention to journaling.

Journaling

I understand that you may already be journaling. That is, putting things down on paper as a record or thought process. You may also know, have heard of or read about therapists who instruct their clients to use it in their practices. You may also know it as something writers do to clear their thoughts or to jump-start their own creative juices. These are all valid uses for journaling.

Have you ever been part of a brainstorming session? (Besides the last exercise.) If you have, you know this is where a group of people gather and work on a common problem or theme. All ideas are written down regardless of how good or bad anyone thinks they are. There are no judgments, no comments or insecurities, just words and ideas. It is a creative process, and usually a very effective one. You showed a little of your creative side with your list of qualities and you will no doubt, prove it again, with some new, creative endeavor that you take-on as you grow more confident in your truth.

Journaling has several proven purposes. It is a place to clear the clutter. It is a place to download all of the stuff we have accumulated in our minds. It is a place to release the emotions that have plagued us, to purge us of those conditions that just seem to pop up and get in our way. It allows us the freedom of putting into words those things we would never say out loud. It is therapeutic and creative and often eye opening, insightful and inspired. Should you be like most of us who would not be able to say the same thing the same way twice, it provides a record to refer back to later. It is a very valuable tool, indeed, for anyone who chooses to make use of it. I am hopeful that you will see its value and take it up following this next exercise.

So here is your assignment: Pick a time of day each day for the next ten days. Find a quiet place and get out your notebook and a writing utensil and write. It does not matter what you write, as long as you write. I don't care if you print or write in cursive, as long as it is printed or written by your own hand. No, you are not allowed to type, and you are not allowed to dictate for someone else to write or type. You will find that there is a big difference between typing it out on a typewriter, computer or other device and actually taking the time to pen each word, each sentence, each thought or idea. There are neurons that fire differently when you write than when you type or dictate. Writing brings more of a personal connection between the writer and that, which is being penned.

For example, studies first conducted by Dr. James Pennebaker in the 70's and 80's showed, among other things, that those who wrote in journals about trauma or stressful events and included their feelings had more beneficial outcomes than other groups that did not journal. There were fewer visits to the university health clinic among those who journaled. Those who took pen to paper developed stronger immune systems. And there is much more! Studies showed improvements in patients with asthma and rheumatoid arthritis, a leveling of blood pressure, and all this from taking a little time to download thoughts, fears and anxieties onto paper!

The time of day for your journaling exercise generally does not matter, although many say that the morning is better.

Some find it beneficial to download before bed, some during their lunch hour. Regardless of the time you choose, make it a quiet time, without distraction. Handwritten or printed, it does not matter. Just write. How long should your journaling session last? However long it takes to complete three pages. Why three pages? Because that is about the length of time it takes to download, clear the air and alter one's attitude and/or consciousness. For me, that's about half an hour. It is time well spent in clearing the clutter and bringing about a healthier, more creative and happier you, don't you think? And what a perfect way to segue to the next subject: clearing the clutter.

One more thing about journaling before we move on though; as a means of clearing the mind of the gobbledygook it also sets the stage for a successful visioning session. Remember, visioning encourages a creative flow of ideas for use in walking the path to passion. Clearing the mind of all the interfering worries or concerns of the day helps to provide a means for all of that creativity to flow. That is also where clearing the clutter can become so important.

CHAPTER 5
Clearing the Clutter

W hat do you think about when you "think clutter?"
(Maybe the better question is what did you think
before that last chapter?) The Wikipedia definition is a
"confusing or disorderly state or collection, and possible
symptom of compulsive hoarding."

Wow. I never thought of myself as a hoarder before. But it
does fit with my having way too much stuff. Now, I know that
includes the stuff in the closet. But what about the worries on
the brain, the emotional baggage, the distractions, all of the
things that tend to keep us from moving forward with what
make us feel happier and fulfilled? Do we include these in
the definition of hoarder...I mean clutter? Can there be such
an animal as an emotional baggage hoarder? Yes. The term
is not restricted to the number of paths one has left in order
to gain passage from one room to the next. Think about it.
Have you been stuck (or have you run across someone who
is stuck) in the self-absorption of your woes? Would that
qualify a person as an emotional baggage hoarder? What do
you think?

We already talked a little about clutter when we talked
about the benefits of meditation and journaling. Clearing
one's mind of distractions, fear, useless information and other

"stuff" is important in moving forward with a happier, more creative and fulfilling life. But the concept does not stop there.

Many of us tend to take on way more than we can possibly handle in a day or a week or even in a year. Many of us, for that matter will take on more than we can hope to accomplish in a lifetime, or so it seems. So, what are we supposed to do? We have jobs, bills to pay, family commitments, car and home repairs, school, and many other things to deal with in life. We cannot just throw those things to the wind and start over when it all gets to be too much. But at the same time we need to do something to allow ourselves to flourish and to take steps toward the pursuit of our passion. We need down time to reflect and to enjoy the flowers that bloom around us. Although it already seems like there is no choice in the matter, we can't constantly keep it going on a rush basis. What would be the point: To die at an early age from a stroke or heart attack?

There is a tremendous amount of "stuff" to deal with in life. If it helps to make it more real, (and assuming it won't overwhelm you too much to see it on paper) go ahead and write it down. And I mean everything: Every chore, every task, every duty, everything. Even the stuff you think that you should be doing but just do not ever seem to have the time to do. Then we can talk about the other aspects of the term to be added to the list.

"Clutter" is not only the physical stuff we accumulate in our homes, garages, cars and offices, it is a term that fills our cups to the point of overflowing with whatever tends to bog us down or get in the way of our going after that ideal which leads to our happiness. Look at your list of excuses, for example. It probably includes aspects of your physical, emotional and psychological life, not just the over-packed closet or the tasks that you will have identified in your upcoming life observance exercise.

As I said, (and it bears repeating) when we talk about clutter we are not just talking about the physical stuff. We are talking about the emotional, the psychological, the Ego-based and the physical. Have you ever had a thought that was so unbelievably brilliant you could hardly wait to get started on it, only to find that all of the distractions of "life" suddenly lit up in your brain like a Fourth of July fireworks spectacular? How did it appear? Was it a rush of all of the other tasks and/or promises that you had already committed to? Funny how these things come back to knock you down like a two by four across the forehead when you are just getting ready to make a huge leap forward. Does that mean that you should give up and miss out on the chance to step into your passion? Of course not: What you have experienced is normal. It is that same stuff you have experienced for what seems like forever. It's an accumulation of the fears, the wants and the needs you have developed over your life and which play a big part in how you approach the new physical, emotional and psychological stuff that comes with it. "It" includes those things that necessarily involve the angst of change, your self-image, the company you keep, and a hundred other things. It does present an opportunity, though, to use some of the tools that you have developed over the course of your reading and working through this book. Let's take a look at the following example.

Think about how many people you hang around with that never have anything good to say about anything. How many times have you told one of them something that you thought was a really great idea only to have them shoot so many holes into it that you ended up watching, helplessly as it came falling down from your lofty dreams into a fiery heap on the floor? Take a really good look at their behavior. How many of them seem to live their lives with a dark cloud hanging over their heads? How often do they turn conversations (regardless of the topic) into a "bitch session"? (More interestingly, how many times have you been carried away with the group and joined in?) How do you think your life is affected by all of that?

If you were to sit down and make a list of these people and compare that list to those who are supportive, happy and on the move with their lives, which side of the page do you think would have the bigger list? Which list do you think would benefit you most in moving forward on your own path to enlightenment?

So what are you sitting there for? Make your list and decide the type of person with which you really want to engage. That's right: make a list. But don't just write names. In this list I want you to put comments about the personality traits you see in each of them. Writing it down, rather than just making mental notes, is far more effective in your realization about the person. Making *mental* notes tends to result in the glossing over of the important stuff. So write it down. You don't have to show your list to anyone. In fact, at the end of the exercise you can perform a ceremony of release by ripping up the list and throwing it into a fire. After you have at least started on your list we can move on to still other aspects of clutter.

The next page contains an example of a simple, yet helpful chart to differentiate the people you find as positive or negative. Careful, once you start changing your life, someone might notice and change their life as well. Maybe they will even earn a place back on your list of positive people. Wouldn't that be wonderful: To have a positive effect on someone else and to be able to change the "N" to a "Y"?

NAME	TRAITS	HANG WITH? (Y/N)

Now that we have gone through your list of people (some of them anyway) it is time to assign a different kind of exercise. This one will require some consistency and commitment (like nothing else in this book has ever required--LOL). Hey! Wait a minute! Did I just use a term normally reserved for text or e-mail? Darn right I did. Why not? Is there some unwritten law that prohibits crossing over on the types of print?

Yes, it is true that, as creatures of habit, we tend to do the same things in the same order whether it makes sense to do so or not and that will be part of the exercise. Your assignment is to take note of your daily activities. You should really consider doing this during the week and also on the weekend as your routines will most likely be different during those times.

As you go through your day, look to see the clutter. What are the time wasters? Where do things get bogged down? What projects do you have that you could get out of the way to allow you more time to pursue your passion? What is (or has been) keeping you from getting them done? What causes the feelings of hopelessness that keep you from getting motivated? What keeps you from bringing your tools with you to make better use of your time? For example, I am writing this during my lunch at a restaurant between serving as musician at church and another church-related meeting. I have about an hour and a half. Why waste it if it is something that I really enjoy doing?

Essentially what we are looking for is to get you out of the same old rut and to do it differently. Even a slight deviation from the norm can have a huge effect on one's life. Even one degree of change can make huge difference in the long run.

There is a movie that was released some years ago in which a television weather person awoke one morning to discover that he was living the same day over and over again. (Gee. Kind of sounds like many of our own lives, except without the time loop.) When it seemed that things would never change, he allowed himself to accept the reality of his new life and started to approach people and situations from a direction he had never thought of before. By the time his time-loop was done, he found that he had completely changed for the better. But one of the keys to the story was that he had only a limited amount of time (24 hours) inside the loop to make the changes. I know that we don't live with that kind of restriction but when you think about it, that is exactly our pattern. We live each day doing the same things, reacting in the same ways and, ultimately, giving up on change by doing nothing to make it different.

The point here is that, if we want something different, if we want to experience the wonderful things in life to which we are all entitled, we have to make a choice. We can either remain in our misery or step out of those old, worn-out shoes of the mundane and pointless and take a new path.

Change really is much easier than you think, especially now that you have an understanding of the purpose of that little voice (Ego) in the back of your head. Remember, Ego's purpose is to keep you in a position of safety through its constant barrage of warnings. Unfortunately, this can also lead to a state of extreme unhappiness if we choose to let it do so.

Clearing the clutter from your life means getting rid of those things that no longer serve you in your search for your path to creativity, fulfillment and success. Now you can get rid of all of those things that have kept you stuck, spinning your wheels in the mud for so long…if you so choose.

So, let's take a good look at all of your "stuff" and decide on what to change. Do you really have the time or inclination to hang on to those things that are keeping you from moving in a more positive direction?

There was a man who had always wanted to learn how to play the piano. Unfortunately he kept putting it off and putting it off. Finally, one day, he made it his mission to sign up for lessons and get started. What was difference between the time he discovered his yearning to play and the first lesson? About ten years: In other words, had he started learning to play when he first identified his interest he might have been an accomplished pianist by the time he actually did start. But don't let that give you the reason not to chase your dream. Don't let the fact that you may have "wasted" some time in getting there keep you from getting there. That's Ego's talk trying to pull you back into your "safety" of being miserable.

You know, change really should not be that big a deal to any of us, especially since we are already making changes to pretty much everything about ourselves on a daily basis anyway. We change jobs, cars, socks, friends, what we eat, the television programs we watch and many, many other things without much thought, and without even a hint of Ego's ramblings. Perhaps that is the difference. We know what we do and don't like, whom we do and don't want to hang around with and so many other things. What really gets Ego talking is when we think about changing something more important than what television program to watch on any given night (especially since the invention of the "record" button). But even in the face of Ego's rants, if we use the tools that we have learned thus far, the path becomes less subdued, the light shines a little brighter for a little longer and we begin to notice a newly discovered part of ourselves emerging and helping us through the quagmire. Perhaps what is really emerging is that bit of knowledge, that bit of confidence and direction we experience when we decide to take the plunge into a happier life.

And now for something completely different: an exercise of a different color (to paraphrase my equestrian friends).

It's probably a bit unusual for an author to tell the reader to put down the book, but that is exactly what I am going to tell you now...after you read the instructions for the next exercise, of course.

I am going to ask you to put down the book and do your exercise of observation that we talked about briefly a page or to ago. For the next seven days you are to observe life (yours) and jot down what you find. (You will probably need to buy some more paper for your notebook.) Be careful though, becoming conscious of your daily routine may cause you to want to change it up a bit before you have had a chance to complete your exercise. But then, that's the point, is it not?

So, what are the ruts in which you have become stuck? For example, do you get up at the same time every day? Do you take the same route to work? Do you eat the same foods at the same places at the same time day in and day out? Do you find yourself watching the clock so you can make sure your activity happens at the same time every day? Are you watching the same shows, reruns and all? Do you start falling asleep on the couch (or chair) at the same time every night?

Get the idea? Be as comprehensive as you can with your life's observations, and do it for the full week. It will lead you to the most interesting realizations. But that's not all you get to do. At the end of the week, take a look at your log of activities. How many days just say "ditto?"

Do you see some areas that could use some changing up? That's the point. Doing the same old thing all the time tends to make John and Jane very dull people. But it isn't always easy to recognize when the wheel has gotten stuck in the groove. Sometimes it takes a concerted effort to see the rut and recognize the need for change. But when it happens, life suddenly begins to have color. Spontaneity becomes the order of the day. That's when life gets creative and interesting!

Ready to get started? (I know that's a rhetorical question.) Just make sure that when you put this book down that you put it where you will be able to find it again. A bookmark probably wouldn't hurt either. (Just saying....)

Welcome back! How was your week? I know you have been through a lot. How is your book of changes coming? I told you there would probably be a need for a large amount of paper for your list.

So, let's talk about change. (Did you hear Ego jump in right there?) I know change can be scary and overwhelming. That is why, in this next part of the book, we are going to talk about how to make those changes without getting to that point of overload that made you quit in the past.

> *"It is not the strongest of the species that*
> *survive, nor the most intelligent, but the*
> *one most responsive to change."*
>
> --Charles Darwin

CHAPTER 6
One Degree of Change

Ever hear the saying: Big things come in small packages? I know it's a cliché saying but it is true, especially in the arena of change. Here are some examples of really small packages with some significant results in change:

Water boils at 211 degrees. At 212 degrees, water becomes steam.

If you decided to start at the equator and fly around the earth, one degree of difference between your intended course and your actual course would land you thousands of miles from your destination.

Ever do an algebra problem and forget to change a negative to a positive in the equation? This one little mistake changes the answer. For example: $-15 + 6 = 9$ is a big change from the correct answer: $-15 + 6 = -9$

A jet crossing the threshold of the speed of Mach one (1225 km/h, or 761.2 mph, or 661.5 knots, or 1116 feet per second in the Earth's atmosphere) creates a loud boom. At 760 MPH that jet is just flying really, really fast.

The difference between that last step on the ladder and the step onto the surface of the moon was quite well put: "That's one small step for man, one giant leap for mankind." (Neil Armstrong, July 20, 1969)

While these are pretty interesting facts, the point is to show you how just one degree, just one very small amount of change can make a tremendous difference in your life. The hard part is, as was so eloquently put by Ralph Waldo Emerson: getting "our bloated nothingness out of the way" to a life of creativity, fulfillment and success.

I cannot tell you how many times I have lain in bed, alarm blaring, trying to decide whether to hit that snooze button again, thereby putting off the next step of my plan for yet another day. How many of us have ever decided that tomorrow is really the day to get serious about that diet or the yard or school or any of a thousand other things? But then, these are the choices we make, aren't they? This is why we have spent so much time identifying where we are, where we (you) would like to be, and what has kept it from happening until now. What I also want you to understand is that none of us are going to be able to get from where we are now to where we want to be in the snap of our fingers. (Oh wouldn't that be nice?) There are steps to the process.

It is true that water changes to steam in a manner of one degree. But first one has to get a container, fill it with water and turn on the burner. Then the temperature has to rise, which it only does one degree at a time.

It is also true that Mach one breaches the sound barrier. But that cannot happen without the plane, which requires a pilot who had to learn how to fly something that took many people a lot of time and effort to build. Can you imagine all of the steps that had to be taken before Neil Armstrong put his foot onto the surface of the moon?

I am not bringing this up to try and overwhelm you. That's Ego's job. (But then you know that.) What I want to bring to your attention is that everything happens one step at a time. Someone running a marathon starts off by taking that first step and then the next and the next. Eventually, if he or she does not give up, the last step is taken across the finish line. There is no other way to do it and, regardless of what your dream may be, or how much is needed to achieve it, you can only take one step at a time, have one thought at a time, make one phone call at a time, speak one word at a time. The good part is that, with each step, you get that much closer to what you are trying to accomplish. It is simply up to you to decide whether to take that step or remain stuck in the misery to which you have grown so accustomed.

Want to know how many steps you have to take and how quickly you have to take them to be successful? The answer to that is entirely up to you. Of course, it is always better to start sooner than later, but the size of the step really depends on your comfort level.

Imagine you have small children who would like to play in the water on a hot day. You already bought the wading pool from the local store and all that is left to see those smiling faces splashing around is to put in the water. You have the hose connected and the open end of the hose is in the pool. You turn on the spigot a little and you watch as the water starts to drip, drip, drip into the pool. You know that if you leave the water turned on like this the pool will eventually fill. It might take a week, but the process has started and it will eventually happen. But you also know that if you turn the spigot another turn, the water will flow more quickly and the end result will happen that much earlier. It is the same with your passions/dreams/desires. You can take a small step now (and believe me, I know how scary that small step can be) or a larger step or several small steps or a small step followed by a large step. The combination is only dependent on your comfort level and your goal. The important thing is to take that step. Any step in a different direction than you have taken up until now is going to have a huge effect on your course, the outcome of your desires, your self-esteem and your level of fulfillment!

Remember that one degree of change, in any direction, will result in a big difference at the end of your journey. The other good thing is that you can always choose to make another course change if you don't like where the present course is taking you.

But how do you know if the change you made is the one that is right for the course you want to steer? I think you may already be sensing the answer to that question but we will address it now with a discussion of what I like to call "the intuitive guide." In the meantime:

> *"Finish each day and be done with it. You*
> *have done what you could. Some blunders and*
> *absurdities no doubt crept in; forget them as*
> *soon as you can. Tomorrow is a new day; begin*
> *it well and serenely and with too high a spirit*
> *to be encumbered with your old nonsense."*
>
> --Ralph Waldo Emerson

The Intuitive Guide

We have all been there at that moment of decision: Ego blaring its doubtful warnings of impending doom while, at the same time, feeling that calm tug or pull to move forward despite the noise. One of these always wins out. We always move forward or we retreat into our comfort zone of stagnancy.

Ego and intuition are always there, always at odds with each other and always vying for our attention. The difference is that Ego, as we have already learned, wants everything to remain the same. It wants to keep the status quo. It does not like change, even if it seems like a good change. Regardless of how bad things get or how miserable we become, Ego will always sound the trumpets of the apocalypse in an attempt to keep us from daring to step forward onto that path of change and fulfillment and success. It is one of the primary reasons we stay in bad relationships, why we pass on the possibility of a new job, why we do not walk across the dance floor to ask someone for a dance. But now we know what Ego is, why it is there and what it does to keep us there.

Intuition is defined by the American Heritage Dictionary as "The ability to understand something immediately, without the need for conscious reasoning; a thing that one knows or considers likely from instinctive feeling rather than conscious reasoning." It is that instinct, that sixth sense, that inkling or gut feeling that we all feel almost immediately when inspired with an idea. The difference with this intuitive feeling is just that: it feels right. As Maria Nemeth would say in her book

"Mastering Life's Energies": When we follow that intuition we move forward with "clarity, focus, ease and grace."

Intuition is the seeker of more. It is that excitement we feel when the idea first strikes and it is that calm knowing we feel when we have made the decision to move forward, despite the butterflies tickling our insides. Haven't you ever heard yourself say: "I knew it!" when you had a choice to make and either followed your intuition or decided to go the other way? What happened when you went with your intuition and you were right? How did it feel to go in the opposite direction from what you "knew" was the right choice and it turned out differently than you wanted?

See if you can distinguish the difference the next time you are faced with choice. Do you feel the worried, panicked, sick feeling of a doomed failure or do you feel the nurturing warmth of good, knowing that you have made the right move? The better feeling is the intuitive guide. (That would be the one where we don't feel panicked and sick and doomed.) There is a difference, and we can hear it if we allow ourselves to listen.

Let's go back to that vision you had of being fully, and blissfully, engulfed in the performance of your passion. Remember how that felt? If not, perhaps now is a good time to revisit the visualization exercise. (It never hurts to experience a jolt of bliss to get you energized again.) For me, the feeling is like the weight of the world has been lifted. I am not trying to please anyone, I am not trying to compete with anyone, I am simply doing what I love to do.

There is no worry of what others might think and there is no concern that failure awaits over the horizon. There is no room for Ego's voice regarding my performance of what I love to do. There is only me doing it. Does that mean that Ego won't try to break in? Of course not! Ego is always there, but its voice is drowned out by the comfort and excitement of my living in the moment. And at that moment, my passion is all that exists.

Doing what we love to do seems like it would be a pretty common-sense thing in this world. Yet, how may times do we hear someone say how much he or she dislikes his or her job or that there is no freedom in it? How often do we hear them say they feel stifled, or stuck in a corner with nowhere to go? And how many times do we hear ourselves say (under our breath) "so find something that you like to do," only to follow it up later with our own gripe about our own job? There is an old saying that goes something like this: "Physician heal thyself." It applies to every one of us who has silently expressed jealousy for another's success, while criticizing our own lack of it. It applies to all those times any of us has been too afraid to take a step towards our own happiness. It applies to all of those times any of us has allowed ourselves to be stuck in our past, allowed Ego to convince us of our own inability to succeed or decided that the status quo is better than the chance of failing.

The saying is personal. It applies to each of us, individually. Why? Because each of us is the only one who can effect change in our own life. We are the only ones who can control our reaction to any given situation.

To make this even more personal, you are the only one who can decide what you are or are not going to do at any given moment. They are your words that come out of your mouth and your thoughts that you have in your head. No one can control what you do from here, what you decide you want to become, or how you go about getting there. No one, that is, but you. In the end, it is your choice, as it has always been. So, do not try to blame anyone else for your decisions (or lack thereof). It is all on you. If my saying so makes you feel badly, that is also your choice in your reaction to the words you have just read, and no amount of anyone reminding you how wonderfully talented and intelligent and capable you are is going to make you feel any different; at least not for more than the moment.

Remember, you have a choice in what you do. You can choose to beat yourself up for not having taken action in the past or you can stop living from that past and decide to move forward. The choice is always yours.

You have come a long way in this journey of you. I know it has not necessarily been an easy path to walk, but you are, if you have done the work, light-years beyond the first day you picked up this book.

There is one more step we need to address in your pursuit of your new, creative and successful life: It is called forgiveness.

> *"The journey of discovery begins not with new vistas*
> *but with having new eyes with which to behold them."*
> --Marcel Proust

CHAPTER 7

Forgiveness

If you have done the work, then you have come a long way on your path to "personal transformation". You have discovered your past and how to keep from falling into that hole that keeps you locked up in past failures. You have found clarity of mind (or at least are well on your way) and have recognized Ego's cunning nature. You have discovered how to tune into life and you have identified things about which you can be passionate.

Even if you have not done the work, if all you have done is read this book, you have planted the seed for a better future.

By now you should know that, regardless of your past, you can only start from where you are and that every day is another chance at a new beginning, another opportunity for the continuation of something wonderfully majestic. You have learned about fear and how it keeps you at bay (or at least how it used to).

If you are like most people, however, you have determined that there is still something missing. It is a feeling beyond all that you have read and learned. This feeling will continue to eat at you and keep you from feeling complete until you have taken action at the level of its source.

The source? You, of course. The issue? In a word: guilt. Guilt about what? Pick something. No, I am not trying to be difficult or coy, but I will tell you that the solution to this problem is forgiveness. The real question is forgiveness of what and who?

The word "guilt" conjures up a mixed bag of definitions, feelings, and reactions. Psychological discussions include feelings of responsibility and remorse for things done or not done, and those feelings can occur whether or not those things are that person's responsibility.

Contemplating the term on a deeper level, guilt includes pretty much the entire gamut of emotions, each of which can really be tied back to a person's self worth.

For example, Tom sees Larry's new car and is jealous because Tom cannot afford a new car, which brings about feelings of inadequacy, which then starts that whole cycle of needing to take action but being afraid to take action, remembering past failures and so forth. (Remember our earlier discussion of fear and the introduction of Ego.)

In another, seemingly unrelated example, Jane's daughter gets in a car accident and is seriously injured. Jane, in her despair, puts herself through a litany of blame by "knowing that if I had just..." I am sure you can fill in the rest.

If we apply all of this to your life, we will probably find that there is an endless list of situations where the resulting emotion has, ultimately, pointed you back to *you* as the problem. This is why we identify the starting point as "you." But then we should also note that the middle and end points are also you. Remember, the title of this book: "Its All About Me." There is no other "Me" reading these words right now.

Before we go any further, I want to revisit the starting premise of your truth because it is important, commonly disbelieved and often discarded in favor of exactly the opposite:

You are worthy. You are smart. You are creative, capable and talented. You are as entitled to fulfillment and success as anyone who has ever come before you. You matter. You are enough.

The starting point in any process is with yourself, right where you are and just the way you are. You are who you are and there is nothing right or wrong about that. It may be an over-used slang, but it is what it is and you are who and what and where you are. Your past cannot be changed, but you have all the power to make changes from here.

The first change: Forgiveness. The final change: Also forgiveness. No doubt you have baggage coming into this process. Maybe you did not know what you wanted to do with your life. It could be you just did not know how to go about it, or how to get motivated to do it, or how to clear out all of the obstacles, get past the naysayers, etc. Because of that baggage, you became frustrated with yourself, possibly with those around you and, as a result, you may have taken that frustration out in ways that you later felt sorry for. And because you couldn't figure it out, you needed to reach out to someone or something else for answers.

Think about it. How many times have you run into someone who has told you "no" or it cannot be done or that you are wasting your time? How many times have you felt stifled or held back or "put down by the man?" What did you do with all of that anger and frustration that you developed because you were held back put down or ridiculed? Unless you had some outside method of release, you probably did what most people do: You either held it in and kept it suppressed in a place where it has been festering, bubbling and boiling into a muddy, gooey, stinky mess of resentment towards all of those who stood in your way, or you took it as truth: That you have no future and are incapable of being successful. Either way it leaves you feeling unhappy or unsatisfied and sometimes like a failure.

So what do you do about that? In a word:

Forgiveness

We all fail. The trick is to put it behind you and move forward. To put it behind yourself, you have to be able to forgive yourself (or whomever you are blaming for your failure).

I know. If you had just done this or that person had just done that, it would all be different. Unfortunately, you didn't and neither did they. So, what are you going to do? Are you going to allow that excuse of some past person or event keep you away from moving forward to the success you know awaits you? If so, perhaps you need to start over with Chapter One.

But why mess up today with something that happened so long ago? You cannot change the past. The real solution is to forgive: Forgive that person for getting in the way and forgive yourself for allowing yourself to hold the grudge, keep the hate festering and for blinding yourself to the fact that it was done in the past and that your whole future is waiting for you.

By the way, was what happened really that bad or are you just blowing it all out of proportion and allowing yourself to use it as an excuse for what is really keeping you from moving forward? Remember, Ego is expert at using situations to point out your self-imposed shortcomings, the impossibility of change and in capitalizing on your feelings of inadequacy.

So what was really behind those events that kept you from moving forward? It is going to be really hard for you to look at it from the perspective of anyone other than yourself. Remember, you are the only one who can control your actions or reactions to anything, and that includes your allowing it as fodder for inaction.

Remember the list of excuses you put together? Now is your chance to add one final, very important item to that list. In this final exercise, go back to your notebook (or the next page of this book) and list every person, every situation, every thought, and anything else that you can think of that has ever kept you from moving forward, from being happy and/or from realizing your success. At the end of that list, and perhaps on a separate page, write the following word very prominently:

"ME"

When you have finished your list, tear it from your notebook, crumple it, or rip it up, or shred it or any other safe means of destruction that you choose. Then simply throw it away. As you do so, take the time to forgive everyone and everything on that list for keeping you from your success and release it from your Ego's arsenal. Then, when you are done, and this is the most important part: Forgive yourself. It may take some practice to keep in the forgiveness mode rather than play the blame game, but you will find it easier as you go.

One more parting comment before we finish: You are a magnificent expression of life. Know it, understand it; allow it to fill you. Step forward onto your path of dreams and passions. Your life of creativity, fulfillment and success is waiting for you. You need only start from where you are.

> *"Until you make peace with who you are, you'll*
> *never be content with what you have."*
>
> --Doris Mortman

TALK TO ME

An important part of this process is giving yourself permission to acknowledge your endless creativity and that you are unique and wonderful. I say unique because, as you have discovered or will discover in this journey, it is your individual magnificence that is to be celebrated.

Each person's journey is unique from everyone else's journey. Each has its own set of footprints; each leaves its own trail of realization and discovery. But though each is different, each has the same, common goal: to live a more creative, fulfilling and successful life.

You have, in your own exploration of self, been exposed to the many different stories of the people who have passed through your life. No doubt you have had a huge effect on each. Maybe you have also picked up something from them. Perhaps you have tucked away some interesting and useful tidbit of information for later use. Maybe you have seen their paths and decided yours lies in another direction. Whatever the result, other journeys have value because they show us what is possible.

If you would like to share your journey, your realizations and discoveries with others, if you think that your story might inspire others, provide some encouragement or help shed light on life, please send it to me by going to my web site or mailing it to me directly at the address below.

It is often of benefit to have someone help walk us through the process of change. If you or a group of you would like me to help move you forward onto your path of creativity, fulfillment and success, you can contact me at the addresses below. It is not an easy undertaking, this change for the better. Sometimes change needs a little help, which I am always only too happy to provide.

Gerald M. Reiche
It's All About Me
27472 Whitefield Place
Valencia, CA 91354
gerry@gerryreiche.com
www.gerryreiche.com

*"Take the first step in faith. You don't have
to see the whole staircase, just take
the first step."*
--Martin Luther King, Jr.

Life's questions have answers and I know there is a method for discovering both. As an Author, Practitioner and student I have learned to listen and to know myself. I have discovered that the method for finding answers to life's questions is not in some far distant and mysterious land but within my own being. This book is a compilation of my life's discoveries, moulded into a method where the reader can realize that it really is all about the "me" who chooses to walk the path of passion, purpose and success.

I live in Valencia, California with the love of my life, Kathy. We may not have realized the other's presence at Fort Lewis during our Army training but our lives have not suffered for the experience. Now we share with each other, support each other's dreams and aspirations and celebrate each other' successes. We do this while continuing on paths once divergent but that now parallel through all of the wonders that life has to offer.